Dark Roast

Dark Roast

A Collection of Poems of Nostalgia and Reflection

Edward M. George

NewSouth Books

Montgomery

NewSouth Books
105 S. Court St.
Montgomery, AL 36104
www.newsouthbooks.com

Publisher's Cataloging-in-Publication data

George, Edward M.
Dark roast / Edward M. George
p. cm.

ISBN 978-1-60306-439-2 (paperback)
ISBN 978-1-60306-440-8 (ebook)

1. Poetry. I. Title.

2016947641

Design by Randall Williams

Printed in the United States of America

A hardcover edition has also been produced.

For Sherry
and everyone who offered
kind words about
my prior collections.

*The days of our lives are threescore and
ten; and if by reason of strength they be
fourscore years; yet it is their strength
labor and sorrow; for it is soon cut off,
and we fly away.*

PSALMS 90:10

Introduction

Until recently I had always been a person who focused on the present and the future, without much thought about the past. But now that I've turned seventy, more and more things that I see or hear, or even smell, take me back to something that happened years ago, and it's usually something pleasant that my mind recalls through a soft focus lens. I think that's what people call *nostalgia*, which I once heard Alabama writer Rick Bragg describe as memories wrapped up in a pretty package with a bow on top.

In keeping with my present frame of mind, I decided to put together a collection of poems, mostly from earlier publications of mine but also including a number that I have written lately. This collection includes poems of nostalgia as well as poems of other types of reflection in which people my age engage. Some of these reflections are sad, such as the ones on the loss of family members or the one on the destruction of the twin towers in New York, and some are just vignettes of life scenes that I found interesting.

I sincerely hope that this collection will bring you pleasant thoughts, or at least help you appreciate how great a gift life is.

E. G.

Dark Roast

It's two a.m.
and here I sit
with a cup of dark roast
and a crossword puzzle
piddling away another night
wondering where my life went.

Let Me Have Back Those Days

Let me have back those days
when I could feel the sun
and smell the flowers and the rain.

When every touch was new
and my heart beat hard
and sometimes there were reasons to laugh, or cry.

When I could taste wine
and bread
and the love on your mouth.

When getting old
was something
other people did.

Midnight Coffee

It was twenty after three
and there once more were we
trying to find eternal youth
sitting in a vinyl booth
in an all-night diner,
being served by a waitress
with her best years behind her.

The usual suspects slunk through the doors
punks and drunks, and pimps and whores
but they only added texture
and color to the picture
of our haven for the lost and weary
with their eyes and souls gone bleary
from every sort of human excess
with no regard for what comes next.

I don't know how many cups of midnight coffee
have been drunk by Bill and me
over the years of our affinity
for self-examination in very wee
hours of the night, roaming empty city streets
while righteous folks were home asleep.

In our many nights of midnight coffee
there's no remembering all the things we
talked about—from women to war
to there's no way that we'd die poor

or leave no mark behind us
before the reaper could find us.

Now our midnight coffee talks have dwindled
But every one we have still kindles
All those same old pangs of wondering
that have always kept us pondering
what the hell is it all about
and how long will it be till we find out.

Shades of Black and White and Gray

*The bonds that unite another person to ourself
exist only in our mind. Memory as it grows fainter
relaxes them and notwithstanding the illusion by
which we would fain be cheated and with which,
out of love, friendship, politeness, deference, duty,
we cheat other people, we exist alone . . .*
— MARCEL PROUST

Spread out around the Formica table top
in my mother's little kitchen
are family photographs
of many decades.
Some I recognize
and some of friends and relatives
of whom I only have
a fuzzy recollection.

The funny thing about family photographs
is that they're not just images;
they're memory ships
that take us back to times and places
where everything was different

some things better—some worse.
Some innocent—some not so much
but still worth revisiting now and then.

Someone told me that
you can never know where you are
or where you're going
without knowing where you've been.
And as I hold, one at a time,
these wrinkled pictures of a younger me,
each one tells me its story
or maybe a fairy tale created in my head.

The pictures that are best (and worst) of all
are those of friends and family now passed
for whom there is no now—only then.
Freeze-framed in a four by five
forever smiling,
forever a part of each of us
who sit around the Formica table top
in my mother's little kitchen.

Jefferson and Union

I left something there
but when I went back for it
it was gone.
Time had taken it.

The streets were the same
but they seemed a little smaller
than when we raced our bikes
through stop signs
and Randy would tell us when to go.
We trusted him.

Progress had replaced
the house we lived in
but the others looked about the same
I guess
just a little older and grayer
and not so much alive
as when we stayed up
till someone's mother
chased us off to bed.

There's a field of sand
and broken glass
where we played football

risking life and limb
and maybe lockjaw.

The grassy spot still there
between the street
and the sidewalk
we used to wrestle on
and fake fights
to scare the people
driving by.

They've taken away the old streetlights
we used to shoot at
with our slingshots
but they left that tree stump
some drunk in an old Merc
ran into one night.

If you yell real loud
It'll echo back
just the way it used to.
But it sounds kind of hollow
now.

The Chinaberry Tree

In front of our house
on Union Street
stood
a big chinaberry tree
that served us
in many ways.

It was the lookout tower
for our enemies
of the moment,
whether wild Indians
or outlaws
or a posse
or the Bracewells
who lived up the street.

It gave us ammunition
for our homemade slingshots
and amusement
when we could goad
an unsuspecting counsin
into eating one of the
awful-tasting berries.

Then one day
a big yellow truck
pulled up
and three men
from the City

got out
and chainsawed
our chinaberry tree
into little pieces
and hauled it away.

We spent a good part
of several days afterward
sitting in the front yard
staring at the spot
where had stood
our chinaberry tree,
wondering what
had caused the City
to come and cut it into
about a million pieces.

It was years later
that my mother
finally confessed
to calling the City
and asking them
to cut down our chinaberry tree
before one of us
broke his damnfool neck.

But by then
we had discovered
girls
and it didn't really
matter much anymore.

Crazy Old Women

There were two
crazy old women
who lived in our neighborhood
and walked the sidewalks
carrying dog-eared Bibles
and asking
Have you been saved?

They always wore black
and a clown-face
of makeup
and rumor was
that they used to be whores
before they got
old and ugly.

The Rendezvous

I can rarely hear a country tune
        and not think of the old café
down the street from my childhood
        where the plumbers and painters
and carpenters would gather after work
        to guzzle down a few beers
before they had to go home
        and face their drab wives
and screaming kids
        fighting over which tv show
they would watch instead of studying
        for the school they would
drop out of anyway.

These men with no past, no future,
        and whatever present they could conjure
would keep that country music pouring
        from the old jukebox in with the glass
that was cracked in a fight
        three weeks ago.

On weekends
        they would be there with their
hair slicked back
        and their shiny new shirts

to drink themselves into oblivion
        and maybe drum up a piece
from the waitress
        for after she got off.

Most of the time
        I was scared to go in there
but once in a while
        when it was kind of quiet
I would strut in
        and pick out a table near the jukebox
and listen to that good country music
        that kind of fit in
with the mood of The Rendezvous.

Baby Blue Cadillac

I'll never get out
of this world alive.
— HANK WILLIAMS

North Union Street
Montgomery.
Christmas vacation
first grade.
I was sitting
on the front steps
sun on my face
when into our dirt driveway
drove a new baby blue Cadillac convertible.

In our neighborhood
new baby blue Cadillacs
were as rare
as spaceships,
so I yelled, *Mama, come look.*
She was in the front room
ironing.

She got to the door
just in time

to see the car drive off.
You know who that was?
she asked rhetorically.
That was Hank Williams.

Hank Williams.
I knew the name
from the little pink plastic radio
Mama kept in the kitchen window
always on 740
the Big Bam.

Hank Williams.
From that day on
I listened closely
to the little pink radio
to hear
Hank Williams
on the Big Bam.
I liked his music.

Then only a few days later
a man came on the Big Bam
and in solemn tones
said Hank was gone
that he had died
on some lost highway
in the back seat of the
baby blue Cadillac.

The Ice Man

On the top step
of our front porch
I sit
studying the dust
on the toe of my shoe.

I hear the clip clop
of the horse-drawn
ice wagon
on the gravel street
and feel a pang
of impending loss.

Next week
the street
will be asphalt.

and the ice route
gets shorter
all the time.

Randy Died Alone Last Week

They tell me
Randy died alone last week
somewhere in California.
His heart gave out.
Just twenty-six.

I thought of
all the crazy things we'd done
and almost smiled.

Like the time
we hitchhiked home
from Panama City
got picked up by a farmer
and wound up sleeping in a barn
to be awakened the next morning
by two curious cows.

And when we found out that
Richard was a desk clerk
at a whorehouse
near the train station
and took advantage
of the situation.

And then there was the day
that Randy opened his locker
to show me
the loaded .38

he'd later use
to terrorize
a high school bully.

Then came the day
he said he was leaving
to follow his dream
and be the first in his family
to make something of himself.

They tell me
Randy died alone last week
somewhere in California.

Dogs I Never Had

There was something in the very air
of a small town in the Deep South then,
something spooked-up and romantic,
which did funny things to the imagination
of its bright and resourceful boys.
      — FROM *My Dog Skip* BY WILLIE MORRIS

With so many little mouths to feed
and so little coming in
we never had a dog
when I was young.

Except that sometimes
in my fertile mind
with eyes shut tight
I'd play with
an imaginary canine friend.

Sometimes a collie like Lassie
would race gracefully across my mind
sleek coat glistening
and she would tug on my sleeve
and pull me to where
I'd reach deep into an abandoned well

and scoop a two-year-old
from certain death.

Other days a sturdy shepherd
like Rin Tin Tin
would bound into my dream
and we would
throw our bodies
into the unsuspecting knees
of escaping bank robbers

Who'd go sliding
face first
into the street
where we would lift their guns
from stunned hands
and hold them
for the FBI.

Then there were days when
struck down by spring fever
I would only want to lie
in a shaft of sunlight
on the front porch
next to an old yeller mutt
who would lick my hand
in dog love,
selfless, unconditional
Dog Love.

At other times
I'd crave a smart dog
like Nick and Nora's Asta
or I'd wrap my thoughts around
a big brave St. Bernard
who'd look out for me
and rescue wandering little brothers.

Looking back
it may not have been so bad
that I was not confined to just one
living breathing dog

For if I had
I'd surely not have been so free
to dream those dreams
of mystic, mythic dogs
that even now
I still hold dear
for the light they brought
into the meager life
of a little boy
on a rickety porch
on a gravel street.

Rocket to the Moon

When I was twelve
without a nickel to my name
I'd hang around the Greyhound station
and watch the buses
coming and going
like great hissing, groaning dinosaurs
branded with mystical names
like *Birmingham* and *Memphis* and *Jacksonville.*

I'd watch the passengers
stepping off arriving buses
and wonder what exotic tales
they had to tell of strange lands
like *Atlanta* and *Tupelo* and *Panama City.*

And then I'd watch each bus reload
with new riders
and as the Greyhound
grunted and moaned
and slowly rolled away
down a dark and rainy city street

It was like watching the liftoff
of a rocket to the moon.

Photo of a Young Woman
on a Back Porch

My father's mother
died young,
of what or how
I don't know,
long before my birth.

For reasons
known only to himself
he never spoke of her.

And sadly
now that I finally have
her photo
found in the attic
of my Uncle Arthur,
a sweet man
himself now gone,
there's no one left for me
to ask what she was like.

I stare at the young
short-haired woman
leaning against
the back door
and in her faded pre-war face

I see hints
of my father
my sister
my brothers.

And in her cocky pose
belying
her plain cotton dress
I see myself.

Picture of an Old Man
on a Brick Street

My father's grandfather died
the week before
I was born.
but I'm convinced
he touched my soul
even though the picture
that I'd always kept
in my head
of him
was different
from the photo
just found
in a long-forgotten
family album.

Still
I'm glad
to finally
see the face
of the man
who used to scare my mother,
a teenager from Deatville,
who'd never seen up close before
a big dark Syrian man

with quick black eyes
and strong Arab hands
only a few years
removed from desert horses.

She later found
of course
he was a good man
who gave her fresh fruit
and promised her
five hundred dollars
if I
his first-born great-grandchild
was a boy.

The End of the Rainbow

I do set my bow in the cloud,
and it shall be for a token of
a covenant between me and the earth.
— GENESIS 9:13

They were three sisters
of the Great Depression
living on a farm in Elmore County
when, after a soft spring rain,
they saw the end of a glowing rainbow
set down in their front yard.

Knowing for sure
that a pot of gold
would soon burst their chains
of poverty,
they leapt from the porch
and ran for a shovel.

When the first hole they dug
uncovered no gold,
they dug another
and another
and another
and another . . .

Until the front yard
was nothing but

a pock-marked mess
of wet Alabama clay.

And as they sat exhausted,
damp, and discouraged,
they began to giggle
and then to laugh out loud
at how stupid they had been

To think that it would be
a leprechaun
who would release them
from their destiny.

Evelyn

She was thirty-six
with seven kids
and a sorry-ass husband
who fancied himself a jazz man
too proud to hold a real job
and only worked enough
to buy his jazz clothes
and gas to drive to jazz gigs
where he played jazz drums
and flirted with young girls
in tight sweaters

While she carhopped
in the December cold
at Cordell's Drive-In
where she served burgers and fries
to snot-nosed teenagers
who left her tips
in nickels and dimes
that she collected in the left hand pocket
of her car coat
with the barrel buttons
and then spent
at the all-night grocery
on the way home
so that the kids
could have food
for breakfast.

Rocking Chairs

On the front porch of the home place
the wind blew
the old rocking chairs
that Grandma and Grandpa
used to sit in
and spin those ghost tales
that kept us children spellbound.

As the rockers creaked in unison
my mind wandered back
to more innocent times
when kids could really believe
in spirits from the other side.

And then I realized
there was no wind.

Grandma's House

I had not seen Grandma's house
for many years
but I was still surprised to see
what was once the porch
piled high in the front yard
and I could tell that it wouldn't be long
before the house would be
completely gone.

The house where my infant footprints
still show faintly in the
lumpy concrete walkway
that was poured by Grandpa
so long ago.

The house where we would spend
each holiday
sharing family meals
followed by drinking and dancing
to my brothers and I
playing raucously in the living room
where furniture was pulled back
against the wall
to make room for drums and amps.

And the noise would permeate
the neighborhood
until the cops knocked on the front door
which was our signal to

start the all-night poker game
where Grandma would cuss like a sailor
and throw her cards
when three of a kind
beat her aces.

As I stood staring
at the remnants of the front porch
I couldn't help wondering
if somewhere among
the boards and bricks
were the Christmas lights
that Grandma left strung up
all year long.

For Pop and Me

I was with Pop
when he died.
Not big to begin with
he lay shrunken and shriveled
from cancer
under a pile of hospital blankets
that couldn't keep away the chill.

Bruce and Wayne
had just left the room
when I reached to clutch the hand
that he was trying to
lift from the bed.

As I held his hand
and in my heart forgave him
for his shortcomings
his chest began to heave
and there was a gurgle in his throat
as he took his last breath.

And for just an instant
I thought of ringing for a nurse
but no.
I wanted this moment
for just Pop and me.

Me and Lady Chatterley

Ah yes, to be passionate like a Bacchante,
like a Bacchanal fleeing through the woods,
to call on Iacchos, the bright phallus that
has no independent personality behind it,
but was pure god-servant to the woman!
    — D. H. LAWRENCE, *Lady Chatterley's Lover*

Her name was Anne
and she was cute
and seventeen.

One day on the bus to school
she handed me a book
and said *Read this.*

And being sixteen
and not too used to older women
I said *Okay.*

That night I read and read
and have never since been
quite the same.

Of course, if I'd had any sense
I would have known
that this was more than literary sharing.

But being young and naïve
I returned the book
as ignorant as ever.

Something Precious

I was sixteen years old
sitting in the back seat
of Coy's black fifty-three Mercury hardtop.

The glasspacks were murmuring
and Skeeter Davis was singing *Something Precious*
on the radio.

All the windows were down
and the spring night air
was blowing through her hair
while she slept on my shoulder.

She smelled like shampoo
and innocence
and I smiled and wondered
if life could get any better than this.

Jailhouse Tattoo

She had a strange allure
about her:
hair bleached too light
pants too tight
blouse showing too much skin
the remnants of a jailhouse tattoo
inside her left wrist.

I couldn't keep from looking at her.

She reminded me of trailer parks
and honkytonks
and the girls
where I came from
and sometimes want to go back to.

The Blizzard

Evening had fallen
on Mississippi's flat belly
but we could still see for miles
as the moonlight lay calmly
across the vast whiteness.

The snow was falling slowly
and ironically
upon cotton fields
softly blotting out
all signs of a road
except the telephone poles
that served as our guides
as Bill and I trudged along
with our load of brightly wrapped
and ribboned Christmas boxes
so incongruous to our plight.

We were hitchhiking
from Montgomery to Memphis
and were halfway there
when the blizzard hit
as we sat drinking coffee
in a country café.

With only Bill's army uniform
my windbreaker

and our teenage insolence
between us and eternity
we trudged our surreal route
between the endless sagging telephone wires
through a foot of snow
in ten degree air.

In our moonlit path
new flakes were dancing
with the undulating wind.
Seeing no lights,
no rising smoke,
we both knew
but neither said
that any stop
however short
could be our last.

At one point
Bill broke the somber mood
by holding up a Santa-papered box
and saying
that if things became too much to bear
we could always fade away
in a Wild Turkey haze.

As the miles blurred
one into the other
we would here and there notice
a white tail deer

staggering in confusion
looking wild-eyed
for something familiar.

Somewhere in the middle of
our frigid desert
we came upon an abandoned store
and had decided to break it into firewood
when a black Chevy convertible
came sliding to a stop beside us.

A lone sailor
on Christmas leave
was bound for Arkansas
from Pensacola
and could take us to the Helena Bridge
if his car would only stay on the road.

We sifted through the snow
for bricks and concrete blocks
and filled his trunk until
the Chevy sat like a mother hen
its tail feathers scraping the snow.

The sailor said
he had not seen another car
except for one
sitting face-first
in frozen creek
about twenty miles back.

We stretched out
and half-dozed
in the warmth of the Chevy
until just before the Helena Bridge
he stopped to let us out
on Highway 61,
the blues highway,
and wished us luck.

We waved good-bye
as we watched the Chevy's
heavy-laden rear end
leaving a deep rut
in the snow
that had begun to freeze
upon the road.

Then we once again
took up our loads
and fell into our cadence.
For miles up 61
we walked in silence
through the still amassing snow
each of us lost
in his own illusions.

Our thoughts
contorted by fatigue
and the sameness
of a landscape

still wavering
between darkness and dawn
were beginning to run together
like words on
a wet newspaper.

Then just as the sun
rose over a barn roof
swaybacked
under the weight of drifting snow
we heard the jingling
of a bread truck's snow chains
and Bill dropped his gifts
and jumped in front of the van
waving wildly
giving the driver no choice
but to stop
or run him down.

The bread truck let us out
at a truck stop in Tunica
where we sat
still shivering
surrounded be stranded truckers
and damp Christmas boxes
drinking heavy cups
long haul coffee
trying to feel our feet again
hoping there was no frostbite.

Twenty-four hours
and much coffee later
we caught a ride to Memphis
with a Korean War vet
who had correctly guessed
that the snow would then be melting.

When we finally
set foot on a sidewalk
in South Memphis
we had been two days
in the same wet clothes
and shoes
and only by habit
were still upright.

Three day later
hitching back to Alabama
in the Mississippi sunshine
was like a magic carpet ride
until this drunk fairy
in a Fairlane
almost killed us
when he passed out
and ran off the road.

His forehead bruised
he let Bill drive

the rest of the way
as he slept it off.

But he kept trying to sleep on Bill's shoulder
and Bill kept pushing him off.

When I awoke
at the sound of a car door opening
my cheek was pressed hard
against a seam in the plastic seat protector
and I recognized the shape
of the tree limb handing above us.
We were finally in my driveway.
We were finally home.

But as with all adventures
we kinda hated to see it end.

A Southern Boy in Boston

Listen to him talk
she told her friends,
pointing at me and saying
Say something.
I want them to hear how you talk.

My first impulse was not to talk
but to pound her
on top of her yankee head.

But then I looked at all her smiling friends
some of whom were quite striking
for yankee gals
and thought there might be sex
somewhere in the deal.

There was.

And from then on
I was downright loquacious.

Near the Charles

It was Valentine's Day 1967
I was a poor soldier
from Alabama.
She was a rich girl
from Pittsburgh
studying ballet
at the Conservatory.

Somehow
our paths had crossed
and here we were
in Boston
leaving the theatre
where we'd seen
Blow-up.
She understood it.
I didn't
but acted like I did.

I started to hail a cab
but she said
Don't.
Let's walk.
It's not that far.

I said
Girl, it's twenty degrees
and snowing

*and my Southern blood
is thin.*

She said
I'll keep you warm
and hugged me
to her side
and kissed my cheek.
Her lips were cold
but soft.

*Let's go see
if the river's iced over*
she said
pulling me, shivering,
toward the Charles.

As we neared the water's edge
the snow increased,
reminding me
of one of those
Christmas paperweights
with the plastic snowflakes inside
falling
on a tiny Santa sleigh.

Look here
she said
falling backwards
into a pile of freshly fallen snow
flapping her arms

to make angel wings
and then beckoning me
to join her.

Leaving my senses
for a spell
I fell beside her
and made my own angel wings.

And then she rolled over on me
and licked the snowflakes
from my chin
and kissed my frozen mouth
with hers.

Espresso Evenings

I saw the best minds of my generation destroyed by
madness, starving, hysterical naked.
Dragging themselves through the negro streets at dawn
looking for an angry fix . . .
— FROM *Howl* BY ALLEN GINSBERG

The Village was ripe then
with the spirit
of the Subteraneans.

She was a strange girl
who called herself Starlight
whose ways bewitched
my Southern innocence.

She took me to dark places
in ancient cellars
where there were bongo beats
and espresso machines
and the fragrance of cannabis sativa.

Where black-clad hipsters
would nod off in the floor
as the H kicked in.

Where pale young bearded men
would parade out

one by one
each more morose than the last

To sit on a tall stool
and drone heavy blank verse
into the morning hours
about things philosophical.

Where sometimes one of the icons,
Ginsberg or Kerouac or Cassady,
would drop by
and bless the masses
with his presence
and maybe find
a lover for the night.

Where I
would sip espresso
in the candlelight
and sit transfixed
by the rhythms of the night
and the Zen-ness of the moment
by the irony of a restless generation
of brilliant minds
searching vagrant alleys
for their souls.

Acid in the Park—1968

Lysergic acid diethylamide:
A drug used to induce
artificial schizophrenia.

Schizophrenia:
The state of believing that
you can change the world
by growing hair.

Thank You, Johnny Mathis

Chances are, cause I wear a silly grin
The moment you come into view . . .

Looking back
those had to be
the best of times.

A little Jack and Coke
and a lot of Johnny Mathis
on the stereo

And me and some flower
of young southern womanhood
dripping sweat on each other's
naked body
in that silly place
where you're not quite drunk
and not quite sober
and don't give a damn
about nothing.

In the Quarter

It was around two fifteen
on a Saturday night.
I was at that point of drinking
where I could still walk upright
but where my feet kept trying to
wander off in different directions.

In my clumsy state,
I tripped on a crack in the sidewalk
and almost fell into a small black boy
who was tap dancing
to a strut played
by an old blind Cajun
on a bejeweled accordion.

I stood there a while and listened
to the music
until I started tilting backward
toward a blacked-out window.
I grabbed the window ledge
to keep from falling
and saw the reflection of
my stupid, drunken face.

I followed the brick ledge
to a doorway
then stumbled into
a blue-lit cavern

of raucous music
and loud conversations
among drag queens
drunk tourists
and ne'er-do-wells of every sort.

On the stage
was an undulating
Dolly Parton impersonator
his/her enormous fake tits
slicing through the smoky air
back and forth
hypnotizing those of us
who were paying attention.

I woke up the next morning
on a damp sidewalk
staring up at two New Orleans cops
who were asking for my I.D.

The wallet I felt for was no longer there . . .
nor was my watch . . .
or my shoes.

At headquarters
they found me some old shoes
in the lost and found
then took up a collection
and gave me a ride
to the Greyhound station.

Young Love

It's two a.m. and drizzling rain.
I'm driving all alone
down some
        long
        wide
        straight
        flat
        ain't nothin happnin'
highway
when on the radio
comes Julio Iglesias
singing "To All the Girls I've Loved Before. "

And I remember
what love was like
when I was young.
When love was not a matter
of just your heart
but of every drop of blood
that was in your heart
and every breath you breathed
and every synapse of every nerve.

When you didn't just miss a girl
you ached for her
when she was gone.

You filled your thoughts with her.
You tried to imagine

what she was doing
at just that second
and you fell in love with her
all over again
and couldn't wait to tell her
once again
how much you loved her.

And when you did tell her
once again
how much you loved her
how pale the words
to how you really felt.

When you were incomplete
empty
unfeeling
except with her.

When the very thought
of losing her
would shoot through your soul
like a hot rivet
and suicide
seemed simple.

When the world
would disappear
when you were alone with her.
And making love
was like riding a roller coaster naked
through the stars.

When hearing a certain song
or seeing a leaf on the wind
or smelling new-mown grass
would stop your heart
as you thought of when you
heard that song or saw a falling leaf
or rolled on new-mown grass
with her.

As I drive on through the night rain
I remember that other dreary day
when she told me it was over
and her words
seemed to rip the skin from my flesh.
But I forgive her as I sing along with Julio:

> *To all the girls who shared my life*
> *Who now are someone else's wife*
> *I'm glad they came along*
> *I dedicate this song*
> *To all the girls I've loved before.*

The Lone Ranger

Willie was my friend
when we were nine.
He was cooler than me.
He painted his broomstick horse silver
and declared that he was the Lone Ranger.
I painted mine black
and was Lash LaRue.

Then one day
his seamstress mother
married a rich guy from Birmingham
who renamed Willie *William*
and took him away,
saying he needed to stay away
from poor white trash like me.

Many years later
came a call from Italy
and Willie
said he'd be back home
for the stepdad's funeral
and would like to visit
his white trash friend.

As we drove through
the old neighborhood
Willie, now Will, not William
told me how he'd studied art

in Venice
and disappointed the old man
who disowned him.
But, Will said,
it was all for the best.

He'd scraped by for years
on looks and charm
but was now a big star
in spaghetti westerns
and could have bought and sold
the stepdad.

He said that he once got to play
the Lone Ranger
and ride a big silver horse.
I laughed at the thought
of a black Lone Ranger.
Will said okay
it was a pretty silly movie
with a fat Italian Tonto.

But he sure loved
riding that big silver horse
and being
the Lone Ranger.

Midnight on the Delta

The tinted moon
backlit the fog
sitting in the skinny branches
of the barren Delta trees.

The only sounds
the grind of tires
on the wet highway
and the rumble
of a long freight train
heading south to Flora.

I turned off the radio static
and cracked the window
hoping the cold wind
would clear my sleepy head.

But it seemed that all I'd done
was make a way
for ghosts
looking to get warm
to climb inside
and plant
those weird thoughts
I always get
at midnight on the Delta.

Execution at Parchman

He that smiteth a man, so that he die,
shall he be surely put to death.
— GENESIS 21:12

The moon was crying
in the Delta night,
a hoot owl moaning low.

A bobcat's wail
rode the midnight wind
through drizzle on death row.

His hands were trembling
against his lips
when he heard the death bell toll

As he softly prayed
one final time
for God to save his soul.

A southbound freight
went rumbling by,
it's whistle moaning low.

His mother's wail
rode the midnight wind
through drizzle on death row.

His hands were trembling
against his hips
when he heard the death bell toll

As he slowly walked
that final mile
to where he'd lose his soul.

Confluences

When Slim played the guitar
you could smell the whiskey
on his soul.

Each note cried like a baby orphan
as he played he country blues
and his gravel voice told tales
of wine, women, and woe.

Thirty years on a prison farm
left him permanently incarcerated
even with a pardon from the governor
who used to hang out in backwater joints
with his cheap mistresses
and bad habits

Where he'd listen to Slim
till daylight
when they'd roll him up
into a State limousine
and deliver him
to the mansion

While Slim and fifth of Jim Beam
hitched a ride with a waitress
to his rented rundown trailer
on the back edge
of a cotton field.

Hillbilly Heaven

The juke joint smell
     of stale beer
     and cheap cologne
clings to blue smoke floating
like fog from an old horror movie.

On the bandstand
     six coked-out cowboys
     playing Mustang Sally
     without listening.

On the dance floor
     skinny rednecks in Garth shirts
     having rock and roll spasms
     with chubby country girls
     who strain the seams
     of mock designer jeans
     or slow dancing
     with double butt-locks.

At the bar
     with a half-drunk Jack and ginger
     in front of me
     and a full-drunk honkytonk queen beside me
     I grin and think:
          I'm in hillbilly heaven.

The Lowering of Ears

Babies don't have any hair;
Old men's heads are just as bare;
Between the cradle and the grave;
Lies a haircut and a shave.
— SAMUEL HOFFENSTEIN FROM *Songs of*
Faith in the Year After Next, VIII

I heard they put Jake the barber
in a nursing home today
and it brought back memories
of Jake's shop
where I had my first haircut
and my first flattop
and had my first ducktail trimmed
to just above my flipped-up collar.

Where I once saw George Wallace come in
for a trim and oil change
smoking a smelly cigar
that simmered in one of the chrome ashtrays
on the counter
and fumigated the whole building.

The shop never changed.
Red vinyl barber chairs
with chrome arms
and green plastic waiting chairs
where at least three old men

were always sitting
reading the paper
and swapping lies
and spitting tobacco juice into wrinkled Dixie Cups.

The hypnotic snip—snip—snip
that always made me start to doze off
until my chin hit my chest
and woke me up
to look in the mirror
and see if Jake had shaved my head
while debating with some Auburn fan
about whether Bear Bryant was a drunk.

Dog-eared ancient magazines
and week-old newspapers were strewn
across a worn out coffee table
that was brought in by Mrs. Jake
the only time I ever saw her
or any woman
in the shop.

It was a man's place
where old men warned young men
what life was all about
and shared their hard-learned wisdom.

But Jake's Barber Shop is closed now.
Jake's son ran it for a while
before he got a civil service job at Maxwell
and sold the building to a pet store.

Last week I walked by
and peeked in at the bird cages
that sat where once old men
almost always misinformed me
about who was going to win the next election
except for picking Wallace every time
for governor
and that was no great feat.

Chalk Dust

School days, school days
Dear old golden rule days . . .

A few days before they tore down
my old elementary school
I took one last walk
      through the heavy double doors
      and down the oiled oak floors.

My footsteps echoed
      off the high plaster walls of the hall
      where in my mind
      I heard again first graders
      reciting the pledge of allegiance
      and the Lord's Prayer
      amidst the smell of chalk dust
      and white paste.

Then I remembered
      how the bell would ring
      and there would be a clamor
      of hungry youngsters
      headed for the lunch room
      where they would drink milk
      from little paper cartons
      and eat from thick plastic plates.

And then I walked out back
        into the tiny playground
        where we would play kickball and red rover
        and let out all the whoops and yells
        that we'd held in all morning long.

And there still stood
        the white oak with the tire swing
        where Mary Lou had kissed me
        with precocious lips
        that tasted like Juicy Fruit.

It was hard to bear
        that they would soon tear down
        this monument to memories
        of thousands of innocent minds
        opening up
        to words and places
        where they'd never been before

Just so that trickster Progress
        can build a big box
        of glass and steel
        which when its course has run
        will be mourned
        by nobody.

Grandpa's Guitar

Amazing grace
how sweet the sound
that saved a wretch like me.

When I was a boy
it didn't look like anything special
to me.
Just an old Silvertone 6-string acoustic
probably mail-ordered
from a Sears Roebuck catalog.

The finish worn through
where Grandpa's flannel shirt
had rubbed against the front.

The back a little warped
from being caught
in a rain storm
that hit the Fourth of July barbeque.

A little crack in the neck
from when Grandpa
whacked a drunk upside the head.

But as I grew older
I learned that
Grandpa had set in
with Hank Williams

when he played
the Bullock County Barn Dance
one Saturday night.

And he'd loaned the Silvertone
to Mother Maybelle
one day
when her guitar
stripped a tuning key.

And Grandpa
on occasion
would get liquored up
and go down
to Willie Brown's shot house
and play the blues.
Rumor is
he once backed up Elmore James.

But every Sunday
he'd clean up
his hungover self
and play gospel
at the Mt. Olive Baptist Church.

The oldtimers tell me that
he played "Amazing Grace"
like an angel.

I own the Silvertone now
and I've played it every place
from Proud Larry's in Oxford

to the Berklee School of Music
where I did a lecture
on hill country blues.

But my favorite times
with the old guitar
are when I sit under
the big oak tree
on the home place
and play "Amazing Grace"
for just Grandpa and me.

Rock of Ages

Rock of Ages, cleft for me.
Let me hide myself in thee.

Desolate
I find myself alone
in a whitewashed country church
with black hymnbooks
in racks in back
of wooden pews
worn slick
from fresh pressed
Sunday-go-to-meeting pants
and stiff-starched
cotton skirts.

The site
of solemn rites
from baptisms
to weddings
to that final ride
by six good men
after the preacher's eulogy
of a you who never was
but maybe could have been.

The smell
of oiled pine floors
baked by years
of morning sun

streaming through
a stained glass Jesus
whose robe has faded pink.

In the corner
a worn organ
that for more Sundays
than I have lived
has led the flock
in *Rock of Ages*
and called to the preacher's waiting arms
those whose hearts are heavy laden.

This afternoon
I sit alone in a back pew
where I finally find peace
in the face of
He whose eyes follow me
whose hands reach out to me
from an old painting
that has hung between the windows
for as long as I can remember.

To Study God

God is of infinite substance.
— ST. JOHN OF DAMASCUS

To study God
by hearing
one religion

Is to to study music
by hearing
one song.

Close Encounter at Walmart

It had been thirty years since I'd seen her
and I wouldn't have recognized her
except that her dark grey eyes
were still like no others I'd even seen.

For just an instant
my heart banged against my chest
the way it used to
and then
she slowly walked away
without a hint of who I was.

And I noticed that
just like me
she'd gotten old and gray
and fat and worn out.

And from then on
I hated her
for getting old and gray
and fat and worn out

And spoiling
the only dream
that I had left.

Miss Liberty

Give me your tired, your poor,
your huddled masses yearning to be free,
the wretched refuse of your teeming shore.
Send these, the homeless, tempest-tost to me.
I lift my lamp beside the golden door.

Flying into New York from Boston
I see Miss Liberty
piercing the early morning fog
with her torch of freedom

And as the sun gleams
off her copper face
I have this eerie feeling
of familial *déjà vu*

As I think of how my great-grandfather
and great-grandmother
would have felt
seventy years before

When as teenagers
they had sailed on separate ships
into New York City

from the old country
not speaking or reading English

And met on Ellis Island
where their family names
were Americanized, sterilized.

But they didn't care
because they had seen Miss Liberty
and everything would be just fine.

They had relatives in Ohio
and Alabama
and they would soon be
Americans

And drive big shiny American cars
and wave as they passed by
with their heads tilted back
and hair blowing in the wind

Laughing big American laughs
and smoking American cigarettes
and drinking American whiskey
from silver flasks.

What adventure they must have felt
lay before them
and wonderment the likes of which
I'll never have the chance to know.

And I wish that they were here now
so that I could say
how much I finally understand
of what they tried to tell me
all those years ago.

Death of the Twins

*Freedom itself was attacked today
by a faceless coward.*

— George W. Bush

It's been two days now
but we still can't believe
they're gone.

They'd been the city's pride
standing bold
piercing the clouds
with their magnificence,
their America-ness.

The day they died
the morning sun had gleamed
against their jeweled sides
reflecting in the eyes of
those who teemed the streets below.

But now they lay
in shameful piles.
Shattered pieces
indistinguishable
one upon the other

As brave souls
poke among their entrails

hoping to see
or hear
or feel
a sign of life
but finding none.

Where once the skyline
had starred the twins
there is now instead
a tower of gray dust
and smoke
hovering
covering everything
with death

Permeated
with the acrid scent of
burnt wire
And the smell
of body parts
waiting
to be collected
in orange plastic bags

And tagged and stacked
in anonymity
while loved ones
pray at home.

On this day
the setting sun
paints the dust and smoke

shades of purple and red and gold
while searchers strive
to set up lights
so that they might search into the night.

The concrete grit
collecting in the grim faces
goes unwiped
as they strain to place the poles
out of the way of
sliding girders.

All night tonight
and for days on end
this rhapsody,
this dance of desperation,
will continue

Until one day
the body bags will all be full
The dust all gone
The air as clear
as city air can be

And there will be only
our memories
and maybe a
marker
where once had stood the twins

So tall and proud
gleaming
in the morning sun
opening their glass doors
to those whose days
would celebrate America.

> (*NOTE: This poem was written within a
> few days of the attack.*)

Country Graveyard

The Mt. Olive Cemetery
is just off the bumpy two-lane highway
that runs in front of the
Mt. Olive Baptist Church.

I park on the gravel shoulder
then begin to slowly walk among
unfamiliar gray markers and slabs,
some new—some ancient

Searching for the name *Jacob Vance*
a long-ago relative
who lost an arm in the
War for Southern Independence.

I don't know why I'm so intent
on finding the grave
of someone who I never heard of until last week,
but I am.

I have felt some sort of strange connection
ever since I saw the faded photo of him
in his Confederate private's uniform
proudly holding his service rifle

And the other photo of him
many years later
proudly standing bearded in front of a
rickety frame house

Surrounded by his family
that included a little blonde-haired girl
in a ragged dress:
my great-great grandmother Rosalee.

I know little about Rosalee
but I was well familiar with her apple cobbler recipe
that manifested itself with every holiday meal
and probably originated in that rickety frame house.

As I walk on the wet grass between the graves
I begin to notice patterns of names,
families who are peacefully spending
eternity together.

In the back right-hand corner of the graveyard
near a tall sycamore tree
I find a small, now charcoal gray headstone
quietly marking the grave of Jacob Vance,
Confederate Soldier.

I stand there for a few minutes
taking in the significance of it all
and shooting a few photos
with my digital camera

Planning to place one of the pictures
in the family album alongside the photos of
the young soldier with his rifle
and the bearded old man with his family.

As I turn to go back to my car
I feel compelled to look to my left
where I see broken concrete marker
leaning backward toward the grave of Jacob Vance

And I notice the name of
Rosalee Vance Evans
and from somewhere in my memory comes
the unmistakable fragrance of apple cobbler.

Unknown Rebel Soldier No. 12

As I walk the gravel graveyard path
among the many markers
of unknown Confederate dead
one softly calls me name
as though he knows me.

And as I kneel beside Unknown No. 12
I sense the presence of a skinny farm boy
barely twenty
married only weeks
when duty called him
to a hopeless war.

In a ragged brigade
of unhewn youth
he'd fought with honor many times
before being struck down
in a muddy field
by artillery from afar.

I sense that when he died
the war was lost already
and that he died with
his hand upon the Bible
in his pocket
and his young wife's name
upon his lips.

Turpentine and Turkish Cigarettes

New York City—Summer 1958
Her studio was on the second floor
of an old warehouse
around the corner
from Sal's deli where he worked
making deliveries on a blue bike
with a basket on the front.

Once in a while she'd order a ham and cheese
and a cream soda.
He'd make the delivery
up the dark creaky stairs
to the red metal door
with the sign that said "Art by Paula."

She'd always greet him with a smile
in her paint-stained t-shirt and jeans
and when she opened the door
there was always the smell
of turpentine and Turkish cigarettes.

She was about thirty-five
with black hair and pale skin -
pretty in a Bohemian sort of way.
She painted abstracts for art's sake
and portraits to pay the bills.

He was seventeen and wide-eyed innocent.
He day-dreamed about her every day -
his day dreams smelled of her perfume
and turpentine and Turkish cigarettes.

One day hers was his last delivery of the day
and she asked *Can't you stay a while?*
He stayed that day
and often that summer.

She'd give him wine and Turkish cigarettes
and teach him about art and music
and life and love
and talk about Paris - where the real artists lived.

His family moved to Michigan that fall.
He wrote for a while.
She never wrote back.

Years later
back in New York
he dropped by the deli to see Sal
who told him that Paula'd gone to Paris
about two years before.

Later that day he walked up the dark creaky stairs
to the red metal door.

There was still the faint scent of
of turpentine and Turkish cigarettes.

Remembering Ella

They sat
his mother and he
in his Park Avenue
in what was once
the dirt front yard
of the tenant shack where she spent
the first fifteen years of her life.

The house is gone now
except for remains
of a brick chimney
and a concrete front step.

A battered mailbox
riddled with rusty buckshot holes
sat on a crooked creosote post
next to the narrow two-lane road
where only an old pickup
had rattled by
since they'd been there.

He'd brought her from the city
to where she hadn't been for forty years
unready to be reminded
of a painful childhood
of picking cotton for pennies a day

Of wearing flour sack dresses
sleeping four to a bed

on a chicken feather mattress
always a little hungry
always aching to get away
to anywhere else.

She'd been silent now
for several minutes
as in her mind she saw herself
and her mother
and a little neighbor girl
sitting on the porch no longer there

Shelling butterbeans
into a tin washtub
and humming hymns softly
to themselves.

You know
we never had grass
in the front yard
but we'd take a rake
and make patterns in the dirt . . .
I don't know why we did that.

Ella loved blackberries.
They used to grow in that ditch
right down there.
She pointed to a spot
just down the hill from where they sat.

I guess
we'd better head on

to the church.
I'm not sure I remember
exactly where it is.

For several miles
there were only the sounds
of the air conditioner humming
and loose gravel
crunching under their tires
on the road
to the Mt. Zion Church of God.

She looked off into the distance
and said
You know what's funny.
Just last week
I had finally decided
I needed to come and visit her.

Christmas Without Mary

He stood at the gravesite.
It was Christmas.
The ground was damp, cold.
The wind was freezing his tears
and blowing against the flowers in his hand.

He read the name, the dates.
It was his third Christmas without her,
each one lonelier than the last.

She'd been his first love,
his only love.
There were no children,
only the two of them
living for each other
for fifty-seven years.

Then came the cancer
that drained the life out of her
one day at a time
until there was none left.

He knelt in the wet grass beside the grave
and told her that he tried to sell the house, her house

because everything in it reminded him of her.
But he just couldn't do it
because everything in it reminded him of her.

Her clothes were still hanging in the closets,
her jewelry in the music box
that he bought her
for their first anniversary.
It plays their song:
Everybody Loves Somebody Sometime.

Journey

Art is never finished, only abandoned.
— Leonardo DaVinci

In the barn that was his studio
there were at least a hundred paintings
in various stages of incompletion,
none finished,
at least according to him.

There was the girl whose eyes were brown
then blue
then green
then brown again.

There was the apple tree
that became a pear tree
and then an oak tree.

There was the farm house with the red door
that became a green door
and then a brown door
and then double doors with stained glass.

All the experts agreed
his art was worthy
and several offered him
a one-man exhibit.

His explanation for never finishing a painting:
Art is a journey, not a destination.

And then one week in June
out of the blue
he finished five paintings
and signed them
and framed them
and took them to a local gallery.

And then he finished four more
and then another
and another and another
until there were thirty paintings
hanging in the small gallery
and bringing in gawkers
and buyers from everywhere.

And then one Saturday in August
I went to see him
to bow down to his genius,
to tell him of an article on him
in the local news weekly.

I found him crumpled on the floor
wet paintbrush in hand
beneath an almost-finished
still life.

> *A painting is never finished,*
> *it simply stops in interesting places.*
> — PAUL GARDNER

Doors

As we leave the rooms of experience
the doors of life close behind us
sometimes softly
sometimes quickly
sometimes slamming us in the ass.

~

About the Author

Edward George lives in Prattville, Alabama, with his wife Sherry. He is an attorney and consultant who likes to try his hand at painting, songwriting, and poetry when not playing tennis or softball.

~